MINECRAFT
MASTER BUILDER
DRAGONS

Printed exclusively for Baker and Taylor

First published in Great Britain in 2020 by Mortimer Children's Books
An Imprint of Welbeck Children's Limited, part of Welbeck Publishing Group
20 Mortimer Street London W1T 3JW
This edition published in the United States in 2021 by
Mortimer Children's Books
An Imprint of Welbeck Children's Limited, part of Welbeck Publishing Group

Text © Welbeck Children's Limited, part of Welbeck Publishing Group.
First published by Carlton Books Ltd in 2019

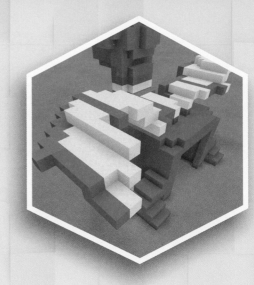

Dragons built by:
Ben Westwood, Darcy Myles,
Jamie Harvey and Jake Turner

The publishers would like to thank the following sources for their kind
permission to reproduce the pictures in this book.

Page 4 (top right): Daemon Barzai/Shutterstock; 7 (top right): Dream
Expander/Shutterstock; 7 (right): Eric Isselee/Shutterstock; 7 (bottom left):
Digital Storm/Shutterstock; 8 (right): redbrickstock.com/Alamy; 8 (bottom
left & bottom right): Eric Isselee/Shutterstock; 9 (top left) Premaphotos/
Alamy; 9 (top right): Ryan Ladbrook/Shutterstock; 9 (bottom left): Hadrani
Hasan/Shutterstock; 9 (bottom right): Tom Biegalski/Shutterstock; 24:
Daemon Barzai/Shutterstock; 25 (top left): DM7/Shutterstock; 25 (top right):
Kostyantyn Ivanyshen/Shutterstock; 25 (bottom left): 80's Child/Shutterstock;
25 (bottom right): AnRo brook/Shutterstock; 38: curiosity/Shutterstock;
39 (top right): Warpaint/Shutterstock; 39 (right): Norma Joseph/Alamy;
39 (bottom): Yuthana artkla/Shutterstock; 52: Refluo/Shutterstock; 53 (top
right): BlueLotusArt/Shutterstock; 53 (centre): Danita Delimont/Alamy;
53 (bottom right): Pavlo Lys/Shutterstock; 68: Christophe Kiciak/Alamy;
69 (top right): Heritage Image Partnership Ltd/Alamy;
69 (bottom left): Everett Collection, Inc./Alamy

Every effort has been made to acknowledge correctly and contact the
source and/or copyright holder of each picture, and Welbeck Publishing Ltd
apologises for any unintentional errors or omissions, which will be corrected
in future editions of this book.

ISBN: 978-1-83935-103-7

Printed in Dongguan, China
9 8 7 6 5 4 3 2 1

Designed, written and packaged by: Dynamo Limited
Design Manager: Emily Clarke
Editorial Manager: Joff Brown

MINECRAFT
MASTER BUILDER
DRAGONS

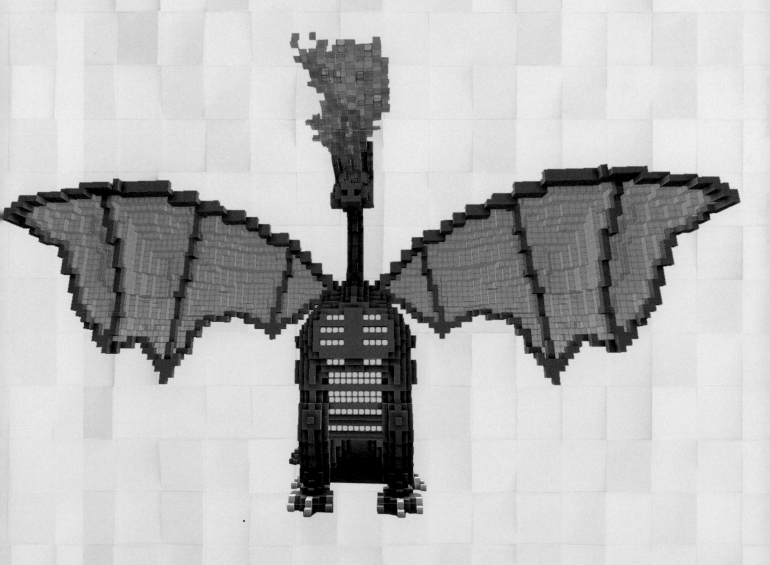

MORTIMER

CONTENTS

ICE DRAGON

COCKATRICE

RUBY SEADRAGON

RAINBOW DRAGON

FIRE
DRAGON

UNDEAD
DRAGON

ZMEY
GORYNYCH

WELCOME TO MINECRAFT
« DRAGONS »

From the UK to China, dragons crop up in myths, legends and religious stories from around the world. The ancient Greeks told stories of flying serpents, as did many other cultures. These dragons don't always look the same – which is good news if you're building your own. You can let your imagination run wild!

« NEW TO MINECRAFT? »

If you've never played Minecraft before, then you're in for a real treat! It's a smart idea to download the game and have a go at playing it before you continue. It will help you to get familiar with the awesome world of **Minecraft**, plus it'll give you a chance to practise using the controls!

Learn how to build this colourful **Chinese dragon** on **page 46!**

BEFORE YOU GET STARTED!

This book is split into **five** fantastic sections: **Real-life Dragons**, **Elemental Dragons**, **Colourful Creatures**, **Myths and Legends** and **Multi-headed Monsters**. The builds range in difficulty from **easy**, to **medium**, to **master**, with the hardest being the **supreme master build**. It's jam-packed with step-by-steps to help you become a pro builder.

ICE DRAGON

NEXT STEPS

This book is just the start, so don't let it stop you from going on to build more of your own epic creatures. Once you've learned the basics from us, you can use your new skills to create more of your own designs.

FRILLED LIZARD

FIRE DRAGON

STAYING SAFE ONLINE

Minecraft is awesome, and we want you to enjoy playing it. Just as important as having fun is staying safe online. Here are some top tips to keep you safe while you play:

☐ always tell a trusted adult what you're doing, and speak to them if anything is worrying you

☐ ask a trusted adult before downloading anything

☐ find a child-friendly server

☐ watch out for viruses and malware

☐ turn off chat

☐ only screen share with real-life friends

☐ set a time limit for game-play

Want to get up close to some real-life dragons? In this section we'll show you how to create critters from nature, from a Komodo dragon to a frilled lizard! But first, let's get to know these brilliant beasts a little better.

《 RUBY SEADRAGON 》

Meet the ruby seadragon from Western Australia. This sea creature is excellent at hiding – only a few have been spotted EVER! Surprisingly, its bright red colour helps to camouflage the spiny fish in the sea, because red appears black in deep water. Male ruby seadragons carry their babies under their tails.

《 KOMODO DRAGON 》

These lizards are named after the island of Komodo, which is one of the Indonesian islands they're found on. Komodos are the biggest species of lizard alive today and can reach a whopping 3 m long and weigh up to 136 kg. These meat-eating monsters have a deadly bite that can send their victims into shock. Yikes!

FLYING DRAGON

BEARDED DRAGON

Flying dragons are 20 cm-long lizards that live in the trees in Southeast Asian jungles. They have excess skin in between their extendable ribs, which act like wings. They can glide as far as 8 m from tree to tree! Males have a bright yellow flap of skin on their necks called a dewlap, while females have a grey one.

These Australian lizards are nicknamed 'beardies', and they're popular pets. You'll know when a bearded dragon is afraid – it puffs up its 'beard' and opens its mouth wide to look big and threatening. Its colouring helps the lizard to blend in with desert or rocky environments in the wild.

FRILLED LIZARD

DRAGONFLY

These lizards are sometimes known as 'frillnecks', and it's easy to see why! When frilled lizards feel under threat, they stand up on their back legs and hiss, showing off their yellow mouths. If this doesn't work, they run as fast as they can until they reach a hiding place.

Dragonflies can fly sideways and backwards, as well as forwards. These critters can glide and hover, too! Want to know the coolest thing about them? There were great big dragonflies on Earth around 300 million years ago. Yep, they were living among the dinosaurs.

KOMODO DRAGON

The first real-life dragon we're going to make is the Komodo! This build is a fun one to practise on before flexing your design skills on the more challenging beasts.

MATERIALS

Komodo dragons are brilliant swimmers! This is pretty handy for when they need to paddle between islands to find food.

STEP 1

Begin by making a big foot and adding four toes, as shown below. Repeat this so that you have two feet. These will be the two back feet.

STEP 2

Build up two legs, then build a bar across so that the two legs connect. We've made the legs wide, just like a real Komodo. Next fill in the shape of the underbelly until it almost reaches the ground.

STEP 3

Create a frame coming from the top of the legs you've built. Now repeat **step 1** to build the front feet, just make sure they line up with the back ones! Build the front legs up until they reach the front of the frame you've made. Then it's time to fill in the frame to make the Komodo's back.

STEP 4

Extend the sides and bottom of the underbelly shape, so that it reaches from the back legs to the front legs, as shown below.

STEP 5

Build the dragon's tail from the end of its back. Layer the blocks to create ridges.

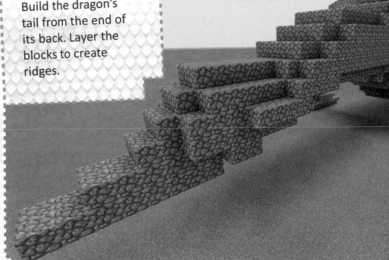

STEP 6

Build the head by copying the shape below. For eyes, add two green blocks with a black block in the middle to each side of the dragon's face.

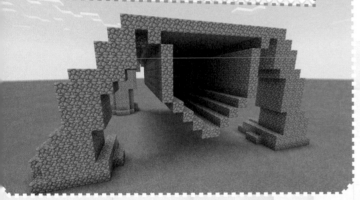

STEP 7

Use black blocks for the Komodo's nostrils, and add a red forked tongue coming from its mouth. Your Komodo dragon is complete – yay!

DIFFICULTY: MEDIUM   **TIME:** 2 HOURS

RUBY SEADRAGON

Ruby seadragons are almost impossible to find in the depths of the ocean. So create your own, and save yourself years of searching!

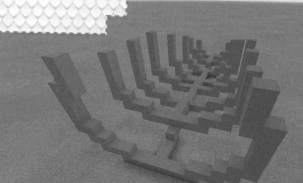

These spiny fish are related to seahorses. They have really long snouts and a tail, too!

MATERIALS

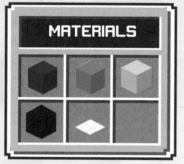

STEP 1

Look at the image on the right for how to lay out your orange blocks in a U-shape. This will become the frame for your ruby seadragon's body.

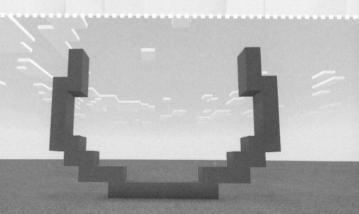

STEP 2

Next, build a long, slightly jagged line coming from the middle of the U-shape, as shown below. Repeat step 1, adding more U-shapes right the way along the line. Think of them as a bit like ribs and a spine.

STEP 3

Use red blocks to fill in all of the spaces between the orange blocks. Now your dragon's body should be taking shape!

STEP 4

Use red blocks to create arches (or upside-down U-shapes) all the way along the top of the dragon. Look at the image on the right as a guide.

STEP 5

It's time to fill in the gaps! Use red blocks, and keep going until there are no spaces. You should now be left with a hollow tube shape, like this.

STEP 6

Now create a frame for the dragon's chest and neck. Build one orange and one red curved line, as shown below. Then add red-and-orange rings to join the lines, as shown in the images on the right.

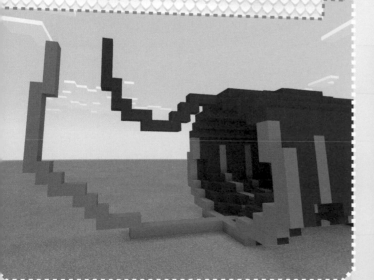

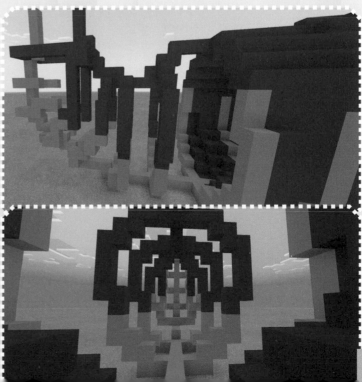

STEP 7

To complete the chest and neck, fill in the gaps using red blocks.

STEP 8

Now for the tail! Build another frame coming out from the seadragon's back. Fill this in using red blocks, as you've done in the previous steps.

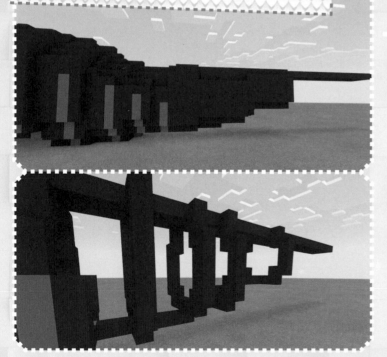

STEP 9

Build the end of the dragon's pointy tail to look like this image below.

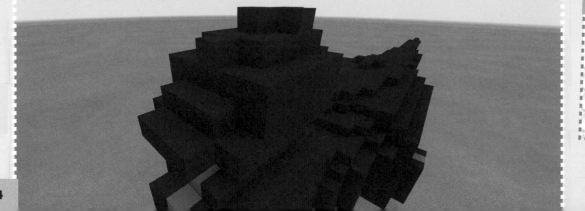

STEP 10

Layer up the red blocks to create a head shape, as shown in the image on the left.

STEP 11

Give your ruby seadragon a really long, pointy snout! Add a few red blocks at the end to make its funny nostrils, as shown below.

STEP 12

Give it some black-and-white eyes.

STEP 13

Finally, build some colourful fins under the seadragon's chin, as well as at the back of its head. We chose orange and yellow blocks.

Real-life ruby seadragons are around 25 cm long.

This colourful sea creature was only discovered in 2015!

DIFFICULTY: MASTER   **TIME:** 3+ HOURS

FLYING LIZARD

Now you've mastered your dragon building skills on simpler step-by-steps, it's time to tackle this flying lizard. Let's go!

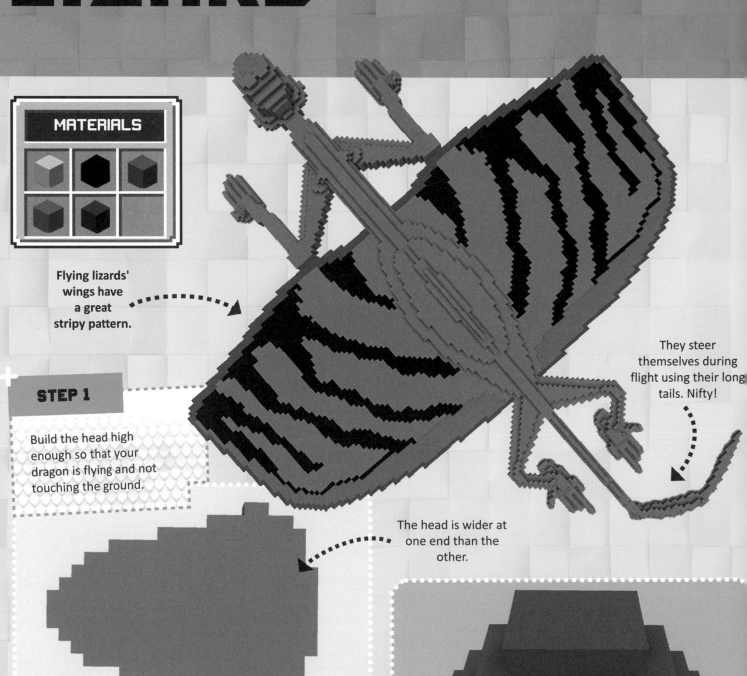

MATERIALS

Flying lizards' wings have a great stripy pattern.

They steer themselves during flight using their long tails. Nifty!

STEP 1

Build the head high enough so that your dragon is flying and not touching the ground.

The head is wider at one end than the other.

leave two 3x3 hollow sockets on the sides for the flying dragon's eyes to sit in.

STEP 2

Next begin to build up the shape of the head using your green blocks. Look at the image above for how to create a forehead.

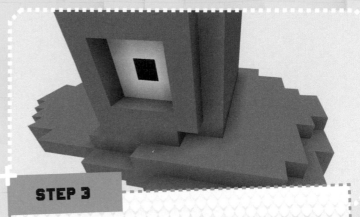

STEP 3

Pop some white blocks into the socket spaces you've made, then add a central black block for each of the pupils.

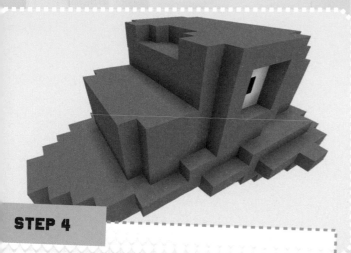

STEP 4

Layer green blocks to build up the front of the face and nose, as shown in the image above.

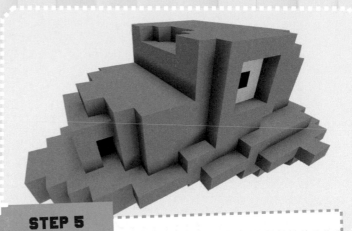

STEP 5

It's time to add the nostrils, as seen here. You can either leave a hole for the nostrils to make them look hollow, or you can add a single black block.

STEP 6

Keep layering up more green blocks until you get the perfect head shape.

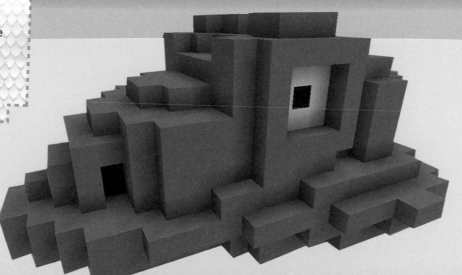

STEP 7

Build a neck coming out from the back of the head. Then add a wider band of blocks, as shown on the left. This is the spot where you'll attach the flying dragon's body.

STEP 8

Next add an even wider band of blocks, as shown below. Keep adding more blocks to form the dragon's back. The small image shows a side view.

STEP 9

Build a front foot on each side of the dragon's body. The toes should line up directly across from the neck. Layer up the blocks to make the feet nice and chunky, as shown on the right.

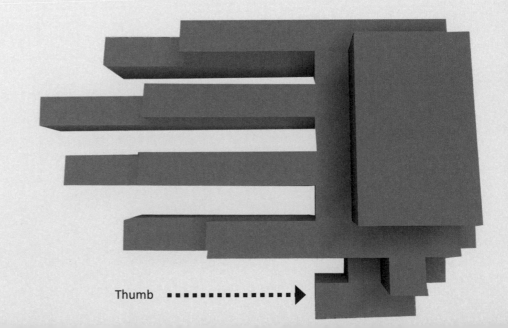

Thumb ▪▪▪▪▪▪▪▶

When both feet are finished, start constructing the dragon's ankles to make them ready for its legs. Use the images on the left and below as a guide.

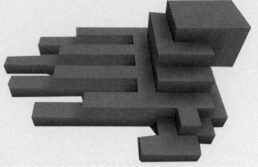

STEP 11

Create two front legs that will connect each foot to the sides of the body. The legs look best if they are bent in the middle.

STEP 12

Use more blocks to layer up the legs until you get the shape that you want. Add more blocks to the part where the top of the leg meets the body, as shown in the smaller picture on the right.

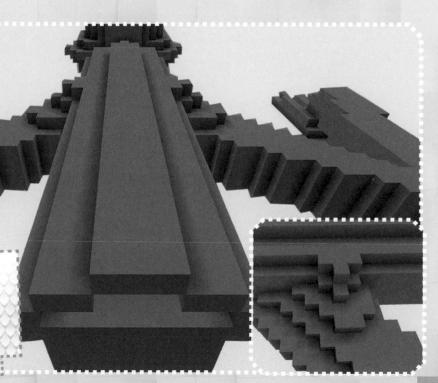

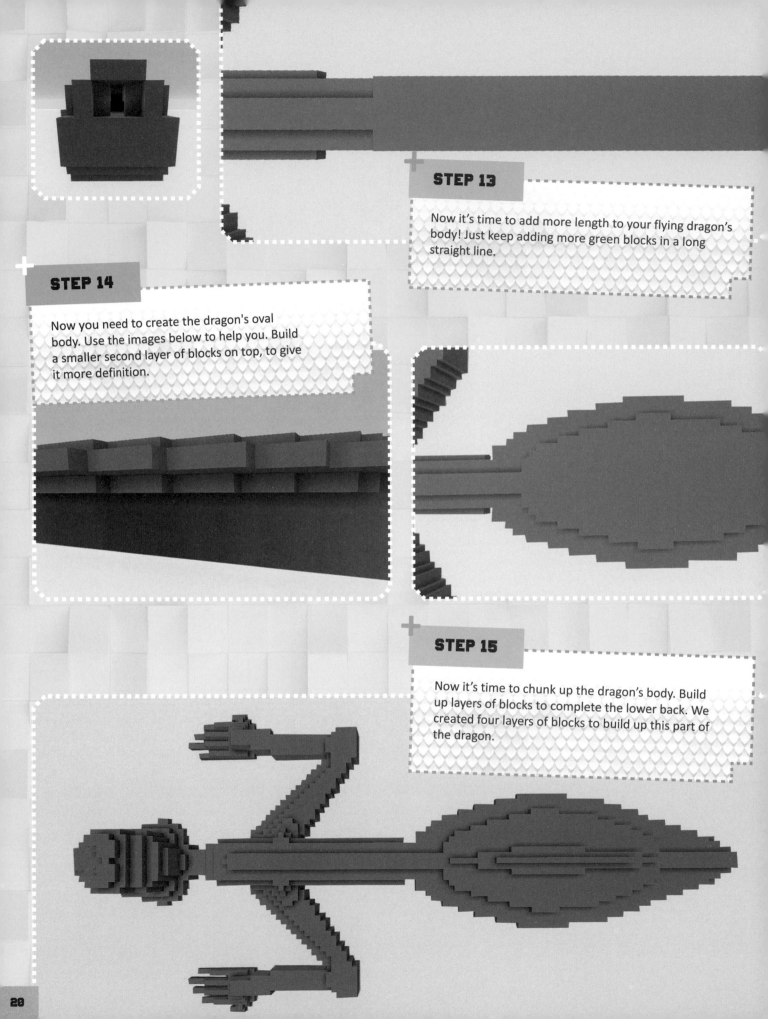

STEP 13

Now it's time to add more length to your flying dragon's body! Just keep adding more green blocks in a long straight line.

STEP 14

Now you need to create the dragon's oval body. Use the images below to help you. Build a smaller second layer of blocks on top, to give it more definition.

STEP 15

Now it's time to chunk up the dragon's body. Build up layers of blocks to complete the lower back. We created four layers of blocks to build up this part of the dragon.

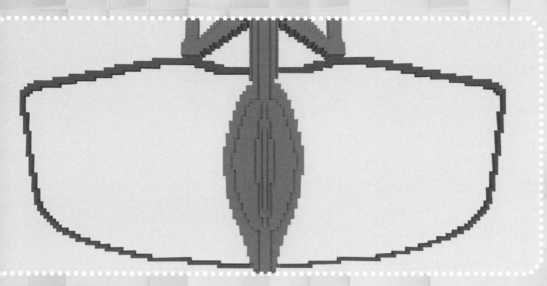

A flying dragon needs a set of wings! Start by creating a frame for them, as shown in the image on the left. This will help you to figure out the shape and size before you spend time filling in all the details.

STEP 17

You've got your shape just right, so it's time to get arty and experiment with patterns and shapes on the wings. We've gone for awesome black stripes, like this.

STEP 18

For the finishing touches, try adding wing highlights along the edges. Bright orange works well with a green dragon.

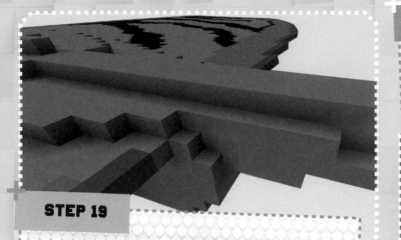

From this stump, use green blocks to construct the tail for your flying dragon.

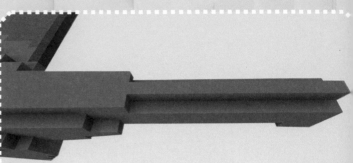

STEP 19

Behind the wings, start to build up a little stump where the tail will attach, as shown above.

STEP 21

Make steps in the tail, as shown in the image on the left. These steps on the tail should gradually reach down to the ground.

STEP 22

The tail should get thinner towards the end. We made the thin, long bit of our dragon's tail curl and twist along the ground.

STEP 23

Next, build two back feet and ankles, as shown in these images. Make sure that the feet are built off the ground so that your dragon is flying!

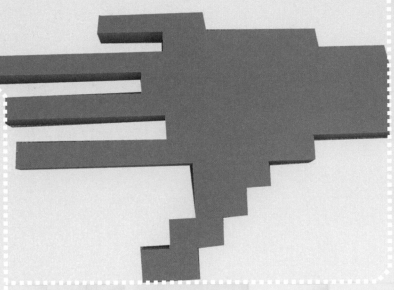

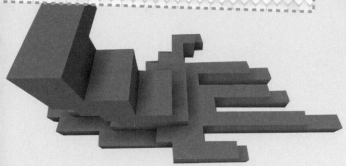

STEP 24

Build up the back legs. Make sure they have a bend in the middle, and then join them to the dragon's body.

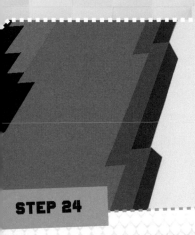

STEP 25

Add some final details and layers to make the legs look more realistic. You're good to go!

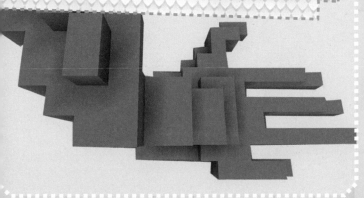

ELEMENTAL
《 DRAGONS 》

This group of dragons is connected to some of the essential materials that make up the world around us. From icy monsters to fiery beasts, here are our picks of the most epic elemental dragons!

  ## 《 ICE 》

Unlike most dragons, this species is ice cool. Rather than breathing fire, ice dragons breathe out air that's so cold they can turn things and people to ice. Brrr! It may be that ice dragons evolved from water dragons during the Ice Age. Some have pale blue eyes and see-through wings. People say that they live near cold seas and frozen landscapes.

This ice dragon is perfectly at home in a frozen wasteland.

fire dragon is the complete opposite of
ice dragon! When you imagine a dragon, you
robably picture something that looks like one of
hese. Most of the dragons that feature in art and
olklore could be categorized as fire dragons. Bright
ed, fanged and fire-breathing, this dragon also
ppears as a zodiac sign in Chinese astrology.

While many dragons are ferocious and feared, earth
dragons are thought to be quite gentle. In some
stories, earth dragons have even let humans ride
them... occasionally! As well as being gentle, they're
wise and powerful. Earth dragons live in forests, so
their colouring helps to hide them from danger.

ndead dragons are believed to be the remains of
ead dragons whose skeletons have come back to life.
eriously creepy, right? If you look closely, you may
ven be able to see parts of its skeleton! Just don't
et too near...

These aquatic creatures have the
reputation of being friendlier
than some of the other
elemental dragons. To suit
their habitat, some water
dragons are described
have flippers and fin-
shaped wings, which help
them move in water. The
Panlong is a famous aquatic
dragon from Chinese art and
mythology. It's said to live in the
lakes of Southeast Asia.

DIFFICULTY: EASY   **TIME:** 1 HOUR

ICE DRAGON

If the thought of an ice dragon sends a shiver down your spine, then this frosty foe is the build for you. It may seem simple at first, but when you add prismarine and ice blocks, it will give you chills...

MATERIALS

STEP 1

Begin by building a blue ice block for the front leg to lean on. Then move onto the four feet and legs. The front legs should be slightly longer and bulkier than the back legs, as shown here.

STEP 2

Create a frame for the body, connecting up the front legs to the back legs. Then begin filling in the body with rows of blocks.

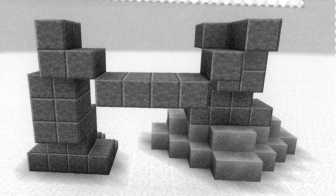

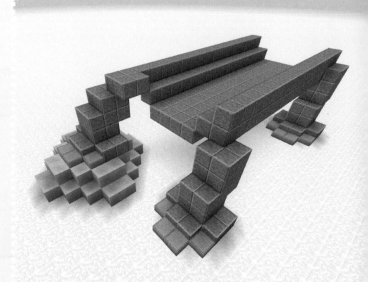

STEP 3

Keep adding rows of blocks to create the rounded shape of the ice dragon's body. Use the image below as a guide.

STEP 4

Now add a sticky-up tail to the dragon's back end.

STEP 4

Start building out a neck for the head to attach to. Leave space for a yellow eye on each side of the head. Then make an open mouth and fill it with a bright red tongue!

STEP 5

To make your dragon look extra frosty, add in some see-through blocks as decoration. Nice work!

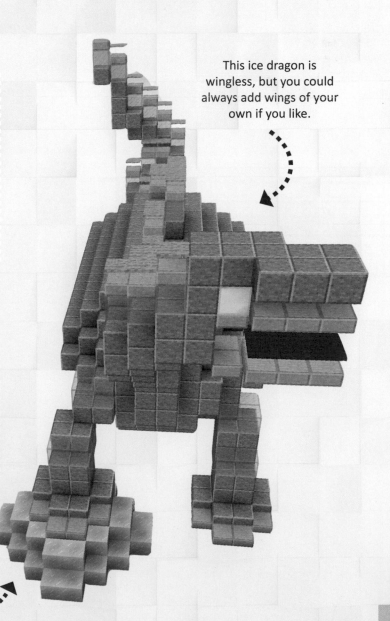

This ice dragon is wingless, but you could always add wings of your own if you like.

This frosty fella is standing on a huge block of ice.

FIRE DRAGON

Things are really hotting up now! Get ready to master this epic fire dragon. Just try not to lose your cool...

This red-hot fire dragon is fearsome in flight!

MATERIALS

STEP 1

Before you begin, remember the head is off the ground. Build up the head shape, adding some eyes and nostrils. Use red blocks to build up the layers on the face.

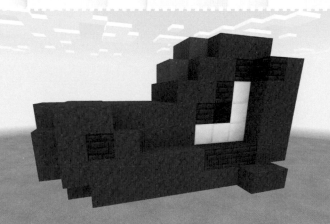

STEP 2

Why not give your dragon some fierce horns, like these? We used black blocks and built them out of the top of the head – a bit like steps!

STEP 3

Now to build the lower jaw. Add more red blocks under the dragon's face, as shown in the image on the right. Make sure you leave plenty of space for its jagged teeth!

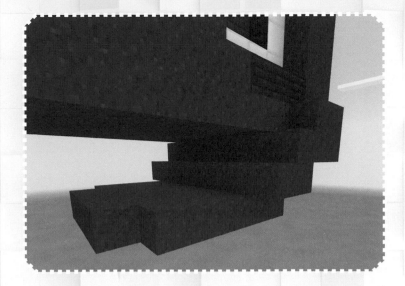

STEP 4

Open wide! It's time to fill that mouth with some big white teeth. For the finishing touch, add orange lava inside. We've put ours in a row between the teeth, as shown below.

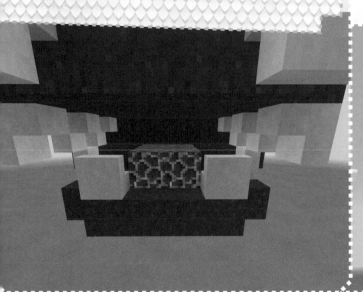

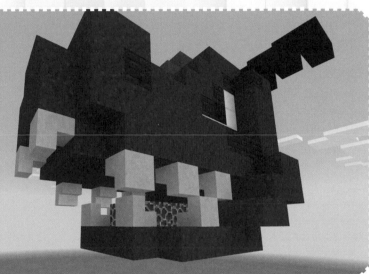

STEP 5

Turn your dragon around, and start to build the neck out from behind the head. The neck should get a bit thicker as you move further away from the dragon's head.

STEP 6

Use your red blocks to build out the body shape. As you can see, we've kept our fire dragon's body quite small – it's a similar size to the dragon's head.

STEP 7

Look at the images below for how to make the front legs. They're short and stubby, with three white toes facing forwards.

STEP 8

Now build the back legs – they should be wider and longer than the front ones. Give each back leg three long toes with white claws pointing down, as shown in the bottom picture.

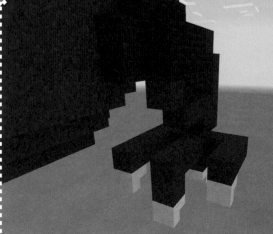

STEP 9

Now, using your red blocks, build out a long tail extending back from the dragon's body. The image below shows you how to construct a perfect wing. Repeat this on the other side to make another.

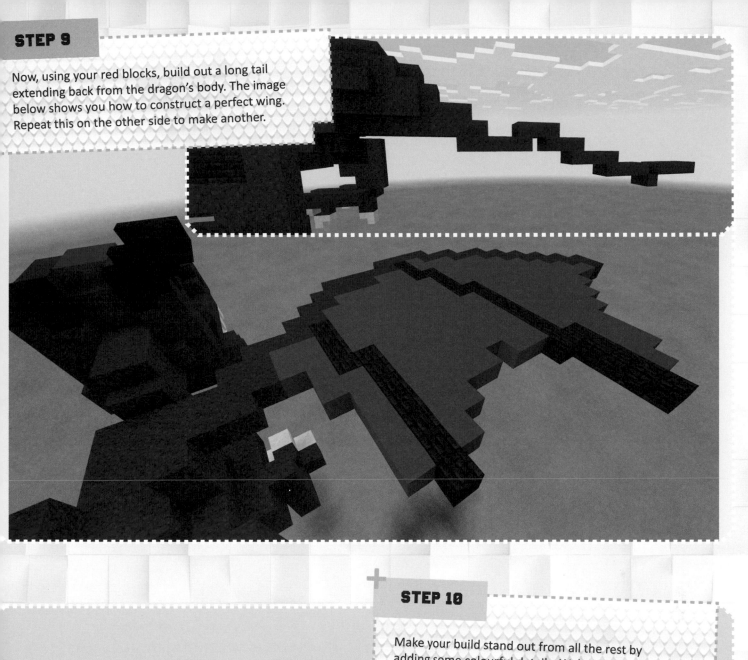

STEP 10

Make your build stand out from all the rest by adding some colourful details. We've used orange and yellow to decorate the dragon, from its head right down to the tip of its tail. Looking hot!

UNDEAD DRAGON

You'll need all your skills and plenty of patience to master this build. Are you brave enough to tackle this terrifying beast?

MATERIALS

STEP 1

Start by building a front foot using grey blocks. Then use white blocks for the three claws, as shown on the right.

STEP 2

Now build up the ankle. Keep building upwards to form the dragon's leg, as shown here. Repeat steps 1 and 2 to create the other front foot and leg.

STEP 3

It's almost time to join the two legs together!
Create a flat structure at the top of each leg.
Then build the base of the back, connecting one
leg to the other, as shown in the pictures on the right.

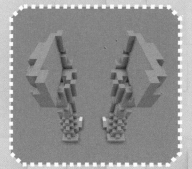

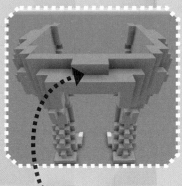

Base of back

STEP 4

To build the back, start by adding blocks down from the
base of the back you created in step 3. Keep building
down until it reaches the floor.

The back
is the same
width as
the base
of the back.

STEP 5

Use these pictures to help you build a back foot at one
side of the dragon's back. Use white blocks for claws,
then build a back leg so that it looks bent – the dragon is
sat down, remember! Repeat these steps to make a foot
and leg on the other side.

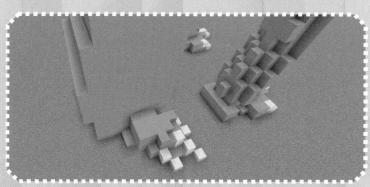

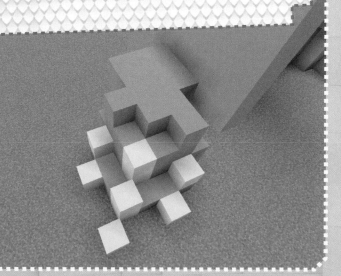

Bent
back leg

STEP 6

Turn your build around so that you're ready to create the dragon's tail. Add blocks in a straight line to begin with, then create a curve in the tail so that it curls round on the floor.

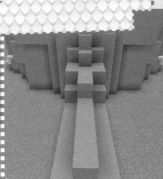
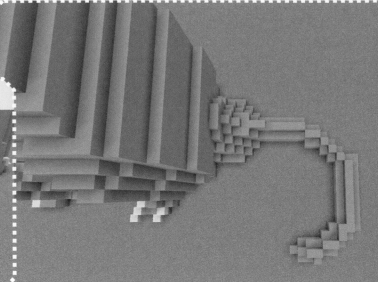

STEP 7

Copy the structures in these pictures to create the dragon's torso. This is the stage when your dragon will really begin to take shape!

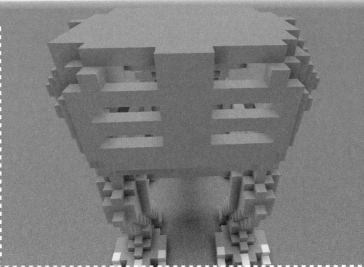

STEP 8

Let's give your dragon some ribs. Start by creating diagonal rows of grey blocks, like stripes, leaving gaps between each row. You'll fill in these gaps next.

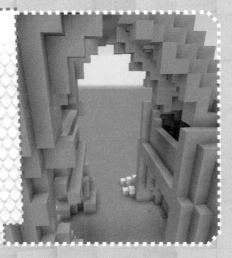

Rows of grey blocks with gaps between them

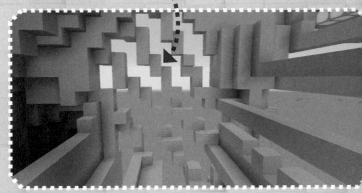

STEP 9

Grab some white blocks, and use them to fill in the spaces that you created in the previous step.

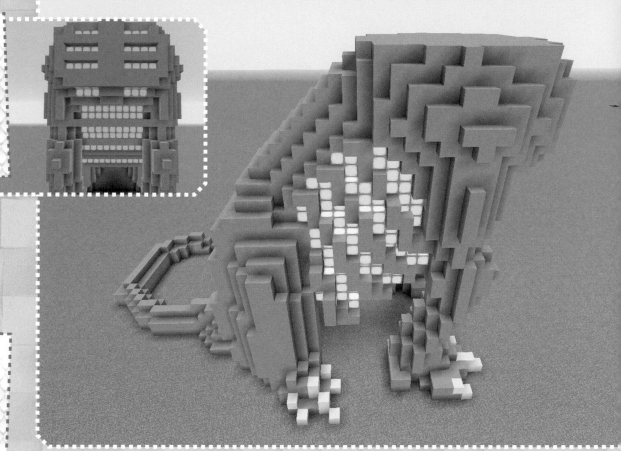

STEP 10

Using grey blocks, build up from the chest to create the dragon's long neck. Each new layer should be slightly smaller than the layer beneath it.

Head base

Lower jaw

STEP 11

For the dragon's head, make a base from grey blocks on top of its neck. Use the picture on the left as a guide for how to build the base, plus how to form the first section of its big lower jaw.

STEP 12

Add some steps coming down from the blocks that you built in step 11. This will form the lower jaw.

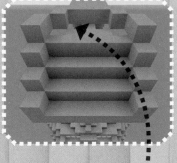

Your blocks from **step 11**

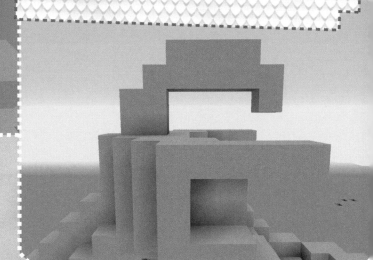

STEP 13

To create the top of the dragon's head, build upwards from the base you made in step 11. Build arches for the eye sockets, and then use grey blocks to form the dragon's snout.

STEP 14

Now fill in the top of the head, using the pictures below as a guide. Pop in a couple of white blocks with green edges for the eyeballs.

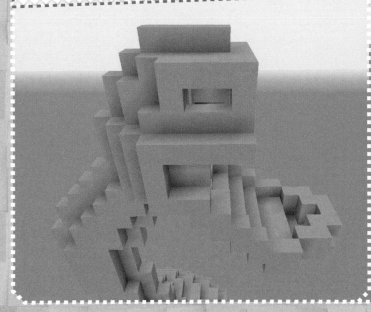

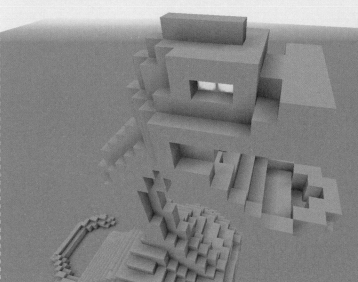

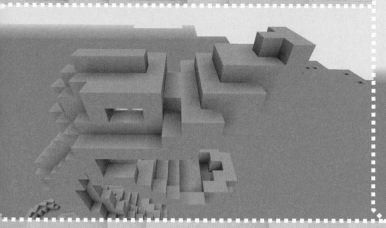

STEP 15

Now for the top jaw! Create steps up from the snout. Make sure that the top jaw extends out as far as the lower one.

STEP 16

Now your dragon has a mouth, it's time to give it a tongue! Use white blocks with green edges, as shown.

STEP 17

The only thing missing in there is the jagged teeth! Add them along the upper and lower jaw line.

STEP 18

No dragon would be complete without an impressive set of wings. Using grey blocks, build a large rounded frame from the dragon's shoulder as shown below. Repeat on the other side.

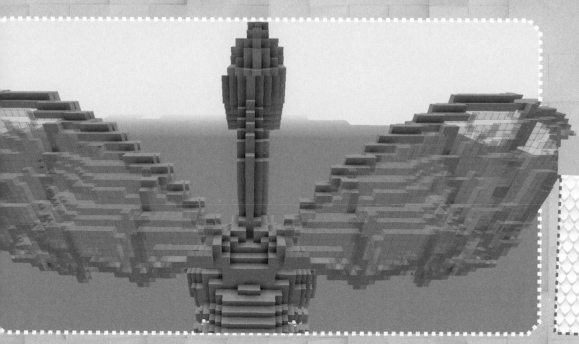

STEP 19

Now fill in the wings with blue see-through blocks. Use them to make the dragon's noxious breath cloud too.

COLOURFUL
« CREATURES »

Are you ready to design some multicoloured monsters? Well, it's your lucky day. Here are some exciting dragons to inspire your designs. Sunglasses at the ready, folks!

If it's strength, power and luck you're after, then look no further – these dragons represent all three. Chinese dragons are legendary beasts from Chinese mythology, and they've become a national symbol of the country. The brightly coloured creatures are part of Chinese art, literature and folklore, and they feature in celebrations and festivals all around the world.

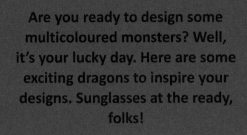

The dragon is one of the 12 Chinese zodiac signs. Emperors in China were once known as 'sons of dragons'.

Long serpent-like bodies perch on four clawed feet.

38

BLUE BEN

rom the shores of Somerset in the UK, comes
 bright blue mythological dragon called Blue Ben.
he story goes that Blue Ben built a rocky track over
he dangerous mud flats and into the sea so that he
uld keep cool – he could get pretty fired up, what
ith being a dragon and all! Then one day, he slipped
ff the path and sunk into the mud below, where he
ed.

AMPHIPTERE

his mythological winged serpent is part bird and part
ake. People seem to have different ideas about
hat they look like, but most agree that they have
ellow and green feathers, and they don't have arms
 legs. With large wings they look a bit like a bird
 bat, and they have beak shaped snouts.

KUKULKAN

he god Kukulkan from Mayan
ythology was depicted as a
ake covered with feathers.
esides being revered as the
od of the sun, wind and sky,
he mighty Kukulkan was said
 be the leader of the gods.

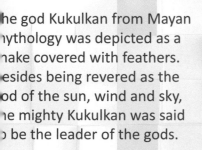

DRAGON MILLIPEDE

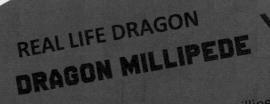

This has to be the coolest of all the millipedes!
This vibrant pink critter is called a Dragon Millipede, and
it's totally toxic. These spine-covered millipedes live in
caves and produce a chemical called cyanide to defend
them against predators. Curling up into a coil is another
way that dragon millipedes protect themselves. These
millipedes only reach up to 3 cm long, so they're
pretty tiny.

DIFFICULTY: EASY

TIME: 1 HOUR

BABY DRAGON

It's a good idea to start small with your Minecraft dragons, so why not get to grips with this little fella? Once you've mastered this one, you can have a bash at some of the bigger beasts.

MATERIALS

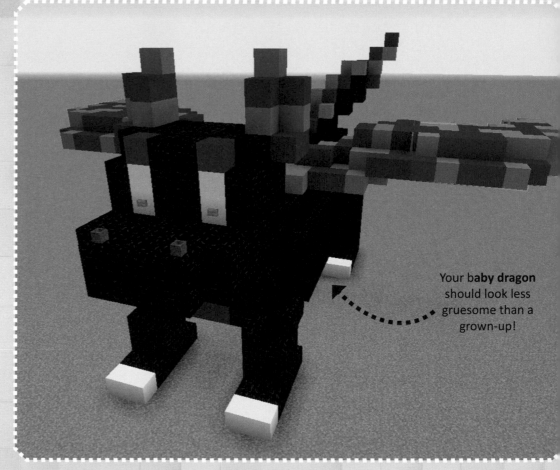

Your **baby dragon** should look less gruesome than a grown-up!

STEP 1

Start off by making a rectangular foot, then build up the leg as shown. Build a second leg next to it, then join them up with contrasting colours. We've used pink and red stripes.

STEP 2

Build two more legs at the back in the same way. Make sure they line up with the front legs, and join them together, as before. Now build up rows of blocks to create the dragon's head.

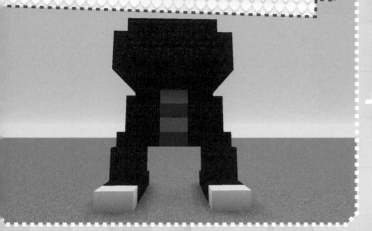

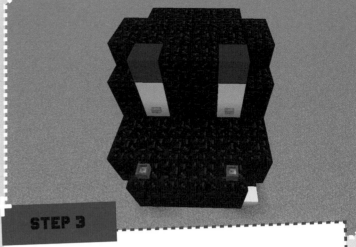

STEP 3

It's time to add some details. Look at the image above to create eyes and nostrils. Big eyes will make your dragon look cuter!

STEP 4

Now add its horns. They will look best if you make them the same colour as the chest.

STEP 5

Add blocks between the front leg and back leg sections to form the body. Then add a pointy tail sticking up from the dragon's back end.

STEP 6

Now for the tricky bit – the wings! Follow the pattern shown on the right, or come up with your own design. Make sure the two wings are the same. Finally, add a row of coloured blocks along the tail, and your baby dragon is complete!

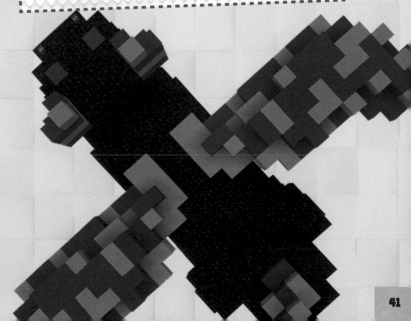

DIFFICULTY: MEDIUM   **TIME:** 2 HOURS

AMPHIPTERE

Arm yourself with the brightest blocks you can get your mitts on, because it's time to build the multicoloured amphiptere!

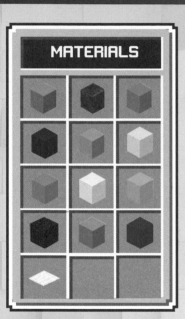

MATERIALS

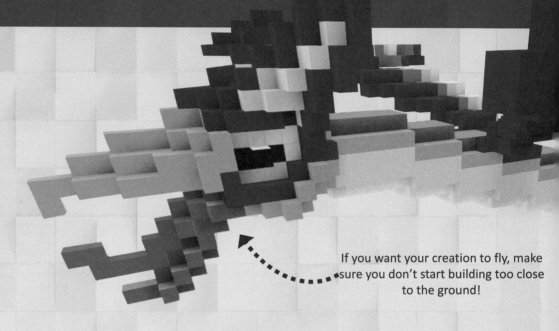

If you want your creation to fly, make sure you don't start building too close to the ground!

STEP 1

For the head, make a purple U-shape, building up around it. Use yellow and black blocks on each side for eyes, then add green as shown.

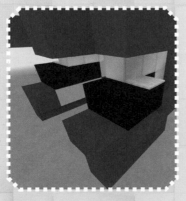

Create a pointed nose and upper jaw using green blocks, as shown here. Start layering up more green blocks to build up the dragon's snout. The picture on the right shows a side view.

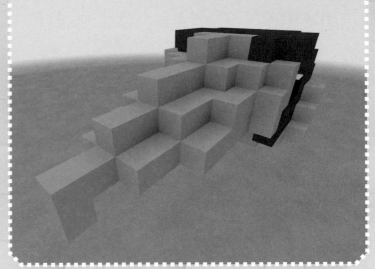

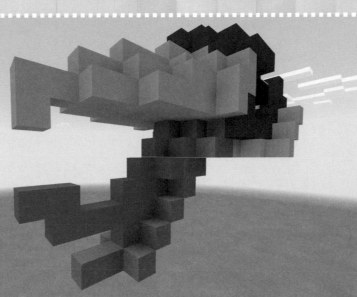

STEP 3

For the lower jaw, build steep steps coming down using dark green blocks. Then add some pink blocks for the long tongue!

STEP 4

Now for the amphiptere's big horns! Create a purple frame on each side of the back of the head – the image below on the left is what it looks like from behind. Then fill them in with yellow blocks, as shown below right. Easy as that!

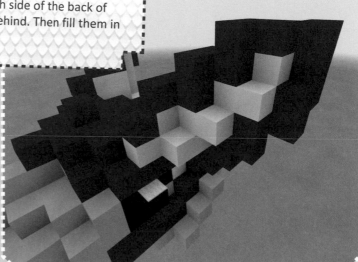

STEP 5

Now use pale blocks to create a narrow line coming from the back of the head, as shown. This will be the bottom layer on the dragon's body.

STEP 6

To bulk out the neck, add three layers of colour from the back of the head. You can copy our colours or choose your own. Keep building, following the pale line that you built in step 5. Now you've created the long snake-like body!

STEP 7

Check out these images for how to build a frame for its large wings. Use the same purple as you did for the head.

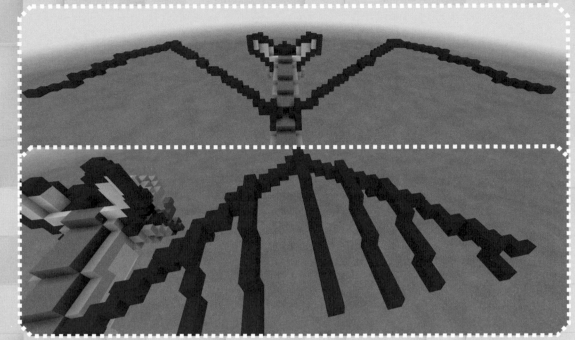

STEP 8

Here is where you can have some fun with your colour palette! Fill in the wing frames with awesome rainbow stripes, as shown below.

DIFFICULTY: MASTER **TIME:** 3+ HOURS

CHINESE DRAGON

Our next colourful creature is the world-famous Chinese dragon!

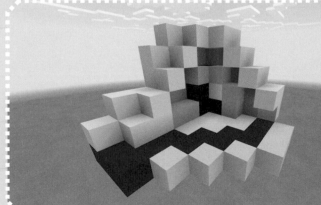

MATERIALS

STEP 1

We're going to begin with the dragon's beady eye! Start with green blocks in a corner wall shape, then use black, white and green blocks for the eye. Add grey blocks for the eyelid, then use yellow and purple for the cheek underneath.

STEP 2

Create the other eye in the same way. Then join the two eyes together at the bottom and the top, as shown.

STEP 3

Use your purple blocks to bridge the gap between the eyes, so that it's completely filled in. Your build should look a bit like this.

STEP 4

Build the snout area and the roof of the mouth using purple blocks, as shown below left. Then add a layer of blue underneath the purple. This will be your dragon's upper jaw and gums.

STEP 5

Build up the front of the face on each side with purple blocks. Then add black blocks for nostrils.

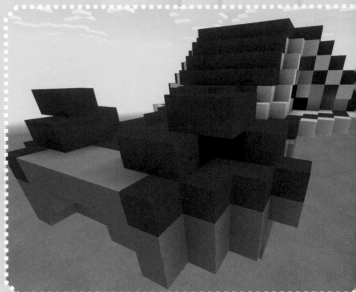

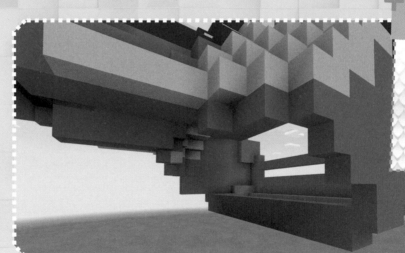

STEP 6

Build up the cheek in yellow and blue. Join each side under the head to create a base for the lower jaw.

STEP 7

From here, begin building out the curved shape of the lower jaw, using purple blocks. Fill in the middle with yellow blocks, as shown.

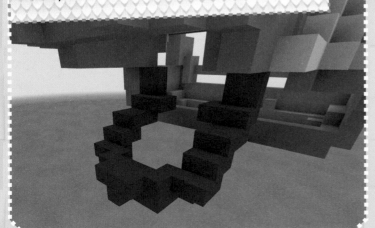

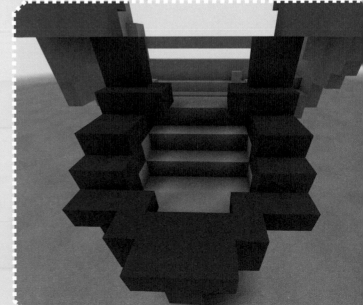

STEP 8

Fancy taking your build to the next level? Lay out the blocks in patterns to decorate its cheeks. Make sure each side matches. Give your dragon long whiskers using white blocks.

STEP 9

Let's move onto the inside of the dragon's mouth. First, add a tongue, and then fill in the other details inside its mouth, such as its white teeth.

STEP 10

Your Chinese dragon definitely needs some horns! Use brown blocks to create pointy horns, as shown.

STEP 11

To get the body shape just right, map out a simple wavy line of blocks, as shown below. Then keep building up layers along the entire length, until you have the correct thickness.

STEP 12

Why not use a line of paler blue blocks for the dragon's underbelly? It will look awesome!

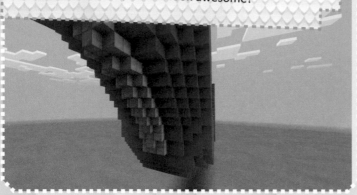

STEP 13

Build a front leg using yellow blocks, coming out from the front of its body. We've given the leg a bend, as shown below. Create some fierce blue and yellow feet with white-tipped claws.

STEP 14

Now repeat step 13 to make the other front leg. Flesh out the two front legs with yellow blocks. Make sure the two front legs are the same width and length. You can position the claws slightly differently to make them look more realistic.

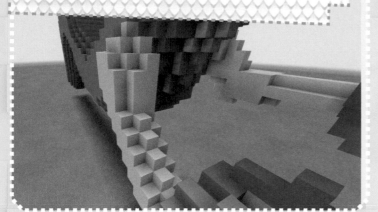

STEP 15

Look at the picture on the right for how to add yellow blocks to form the base of the back legs. Next, extend the legs backwards towards the end of the dragon's body.

STEP 16

Build the back feet in the same way as you did in step 13. But this time, make the claws point backwards rather than forwards. Add white tips to the claws and yellow blocks for detail.

STEP 17

Now build a thick, swishy tail onto the end of the body using blue blocks.

STEP 18

Finally, add some more colour! Add orange stripes to the sides of the body. Then add a line of yellow blocks along the length of its body and tail.

We added purple and yellow spines along our **Chinese dragon's** back.

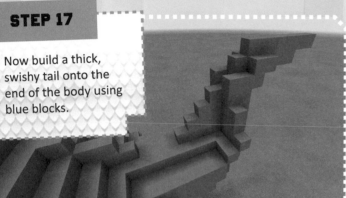

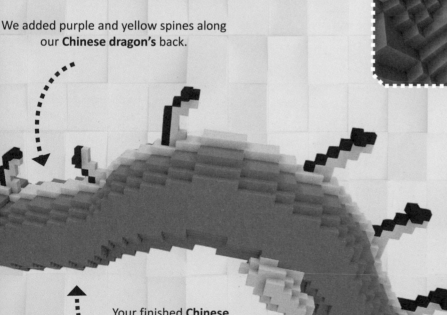

Your finished **Chinese dragon** could look like this, or add your own colourful details!

MYTHS AND LEGENDS

Prepare to be amazed by these fantastic dragons from folklore around the world. Then you'll get the chance to make some of these mythic beasties for yourself!

 ## APALALA   ## DRAGONET

The water or river dragon Apalala comes from Buddhist mythology. The creature is said to be the spirit of the Subhavastu river (now Pakistan's Swat River) and is the basis for a popular tale told to Buddhist children. It is believed that Apalala was once a man called Gangi, who was converted to Buddhism by the Buddha. The story teaches young children that Buddhism brings happiness.

Dragonets feature in Swiss folklore from the Middle Ages. They're much smaller than your average dragon but don't their size fool you! These angry fire-breathers hunt in packs and have enormous appetite. They're not AT ALL friendly, so watch out!

Why not give one of your builds a twisty tail?

Check out the teeth on **Apalala!**

COCKATRICE

These mythical creatures are sometimes called basilisks. The beasts have the legs, wings and head of a cockerel, or young rooster, combined with the body and tail of a snake. According to folklore, they come from an egg laid by a cockerel that was hatched by a snake – weird! Although small, these desert-dwellers are deadly. Besides their venomous breath, they can kill with one glance. Yikes!

AYIDA-WEDO

Also known as the Rainbow Serpent, Ayida-Wedo is a spirit from Haiti. She is the goddess of rainbows, wind, fire, water and... snakes! The colourful serpent represents strength, healing and unity. She also symbolizes the link between heaven and Earth. Ayida-Wedo is married to the sky god Damballah-Wedo. In the myth, the pair are seen as a rainbow over the island of Haiti.

STATUE OF AYIDA-WEDO

BOLLA

The bolla comes from ancient Albanian folklore. According to myth, this snake-like demon spends most of the time with its eyes shut. It will only open its eyes once a year on Saint George's Day. Then, if it happens to catch sight of an unlucky human, it will devour them instantly. You've been warned! Bollas evolve to have nine tongues, spines and horns, plus they can breathe fire. Impressive!

WELSH FLAG

WELSH DRAGON

The Welsh Dragon, or Y Ddraig Goch (the Red Dragon), crops up in Celtic mythology. A symbol of Wales, it famously appears on the country's flag.

DIFFICULTY: EASY   **TIME:** 1 HOUR

DRAGONET

Got an hour to spare? Then grab your brightest blue blocks and follow these simple steps to build this small but deadly dragon...

It has long legs and large claws.

MATERIALS

This dragonet is on the ground, ready to pounce!

STEP 1

Start by building a big, solid blue cube for the dragonet's body. At the front of the cube, add rows of alternating colours to create stripes. Build two bent front legs with blue blocks, and then add clawed feet with white tips.

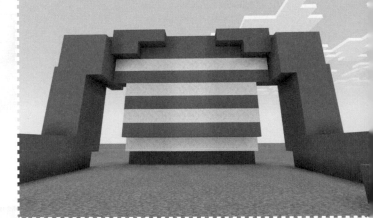

STEP 2

Build a rectangular striped neck coming up from the front of the body. Layer blocks to form the face and eyes, as shown on the right. Add two pointy grey horns on top of the head.

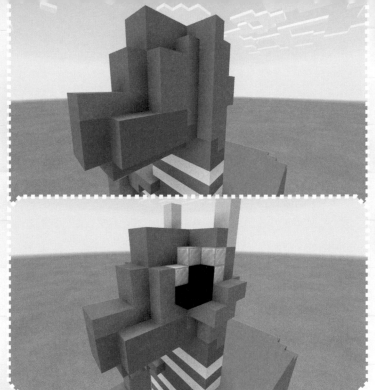

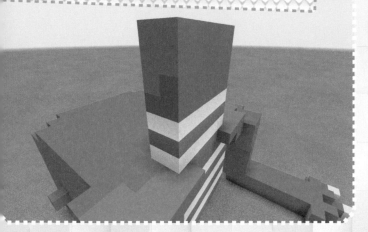

STEP 3

Add short back legs, so it looks like the dragonet is sitting. Don't forget its claws!

STEP 4

Create frames for the wings, as shown in the image below. Fill them in when you've got the shape you want. We've made our dragonet's wings the same colours as the stripes on its body.

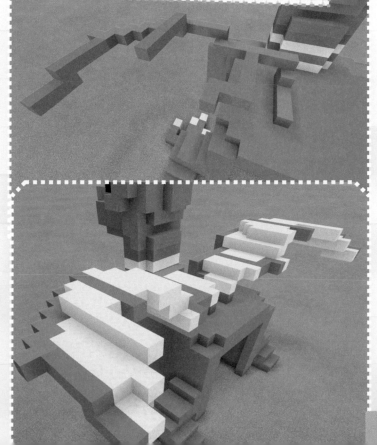

STEP 5

Finally, fill in the back end of your dragonet, and give it a long tail using two shades of blue. Cool!

COCKATRICE

Quick, avert your eyes – a cockatrice's glance is totally deadly! Building your own is the safest way to take a good look...

MATERIALS

The cockatrice has skinny chicken legs and nasty claws!

STEP 1

Start by building a yellow foot and leg. The leg should be slightly bent, as shown below.

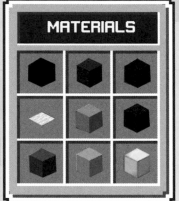

STEP 2

Add some black blocks to create fearsome-looking claws!

For the top of the cockatrice's leg, build up a cluster of brown blocks. Look at the pictures on the right for how to build across to form the base of the mythical creature's body.

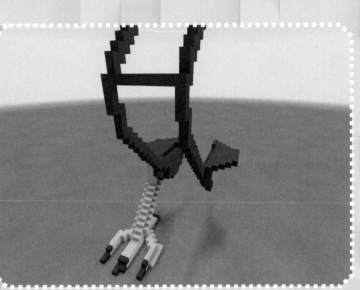

STEP 4

Build a frame for the cockatrice's curved bird-like chest, as shown on the left. Add a base of brown blocks for the other leg to attach to, as you did in step 3.

STEP 5

Using brown blocks, fill in the frame of the body you mapped out in the previous step. Then build the cockatrice's other leg with yellow blocks as before, ensuring it's the same width and length as the first leg. But this time, angle the leg so it bends backwards, so it looks like it's running along!

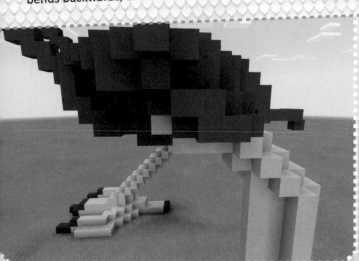

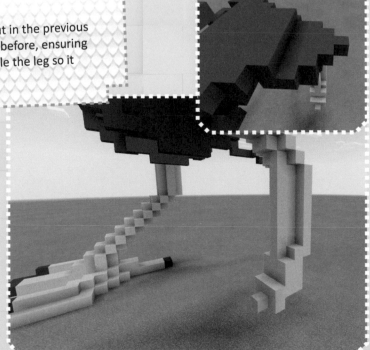

STEP 6

The cockatrice's second foot also needs to bend backwards, as shown in the images on the right. When you're happy with the foot shape, add some of those sharp claws again!

STEP 8

Construct some arcs to frame the cockatrice's body shape, as shown below. Then fill the body in with brown blocks.

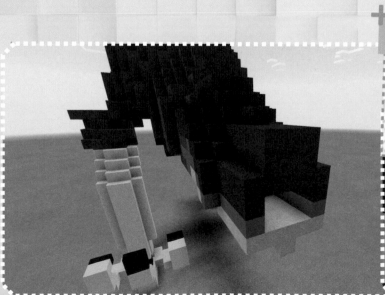

STEP 7

Move round to the curved chest frame that you built in step 4. Now it's time to fill in the cockatrice's chest with two shades of grey blocks. Use the picture above as a guide.

STEP 9

When the body is filled in, work your way down to the tail area. Build out to create the tail using the two shades of grey blocks you used for the cockatrice's chest. Looking good!

STEP 10

To create the neck, build some small arcs, then fill in with more brown blocks.

STEP 11

Now for the head! Build a brown head shape, leaving spaces on either side for eye sockets. Partially-fill these with black and white, as shown.

STEP 12

Build a pointy beak using two shades of yellow blocks. Now add a head crest made from red blocks.

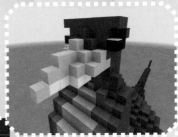

STEP 13

Use brown blocks to create a frame for the cockatrice's wings, as shown below. When you're happy that both wings match, fill them in with some grey blocks... and you're done!

DIFFICULTY: MASTER   **TIME:** 3+ HOURS

RAINBOW DRAGON

Up next we have a dragon that's sure to brighten any day! It's none other than the rainbow dragon, of course.

MATERIALS

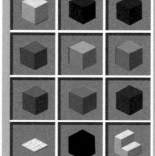

Use lots of **rainbow colours** on your dragon wings!

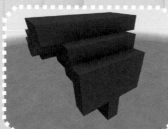

STEP 2

Now for the dragon's long snout! Use more purple blocks to extend out from the front of the face, as shown below.

STEP 1

Copy the top picture to create the purple head shape. Then build out until you have created steps down the front and back, as shown in the two smaller pictures. Leave a space on each side of the head for the eye sockets.

STEP 3

Let's give the head some more shape! Create a ridge by building a narrow strip of blocks down the head and along the dragon's snout.

+ STEP 4

Now build up the nose at the end of the snout. Leave gaps on each side to make hollow nostrils. Use the image on the left to help you.

STEP 5

Now it's time to go back to the eye sockets that you created in step 1. Make sure you have enough space for the dragon's big eyes and that you're happy with the shape!

+ STEP 6

Use white blocks for the front and top of the eye, as shown below. Then add a layer of yellow beneath them. Finish it off with a black pupil. Repeat this for the eye on the other side!

STEP 7

Keep your black blocks handy because you'll need some for the nostrils. Use them as shown on each side of the dragon's snout!

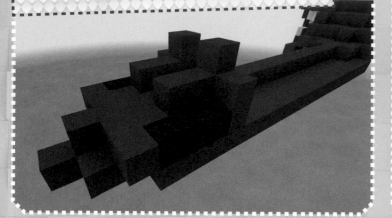

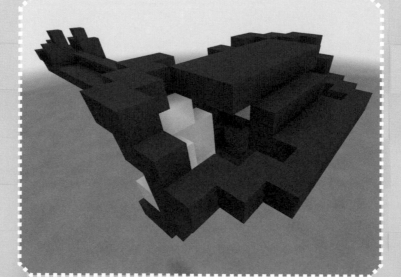

STEP 8

The snout is probably still looking a bit flat, so now is a good time to add some more details. Use purple blocks to create more layers beneath the snout. Look at the image on the left for the shape to aim for.

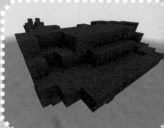

STEP 9

Build up the back of the dragon's head with purple blocks to make it look more rounded. Add plenty of blocks around the eye areas, too.

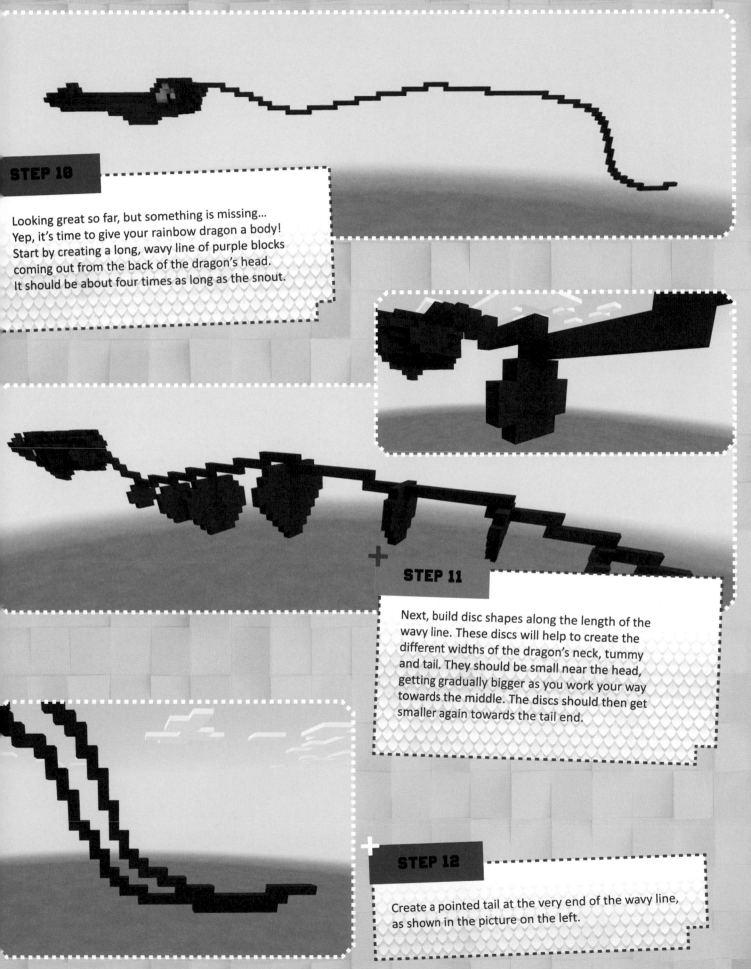

Looking great so far, but something is missing...
Yep, it's time to give your rainbow dragon a body!
Start by creating a long, wavy line of purple blocks
coming out from the back of the dragon's head.
It should be about four times as long as the snout.

STEP 11

Next, build disc shapes along the length of the
wavy line. These discs will help to create the
different widths of the dragon's neck, tummy
and tail. They should be small near the head,
getting gradually bigger as you work your way
towards the middle. The discs should then get
smaller again towards the tail end.

STEP 12

Create a pointed tail at the very end of the wavy line,
as shown in the picture on the left.

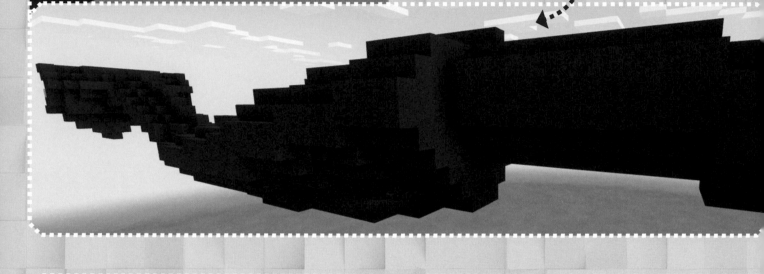

STEP 13

Now fill in all the spaces between the discs that you created to make the dragon's body. They should help you achieve the perfect body shape for your rainbow dragon.

This side view shows how your dragon's body should be taking shape!

STEP 14

Keep layering your blocks to give the body a more rounded shape. Fill in the tip of the tail. Up close, the blocks will look a bit like steep steps.

STEP 15

The picture above shows what the body should look like. You can zoom in and out as you go to keep checking that the shape is going to plan!

STEP 16

Add a thin spike of purple blocks coming out from the top of its head, as shown in the picture above.

STEP 17

Time to get a lot more colourful! Create this fin-like head crest by adding rows of rainbow stripes. Use the image above as a guide, or design your own.

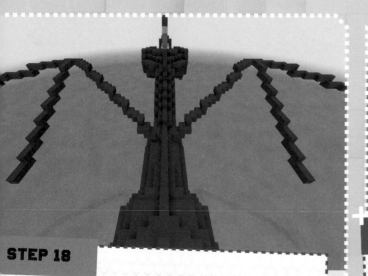

STEP 18

It's time to create the wing frames! See above for where the wings should join to the body.

STEP 19

Now fill in the wings using the rainbow colours, as you did on the head crest. Put the colours in the same order to make it look awesome!

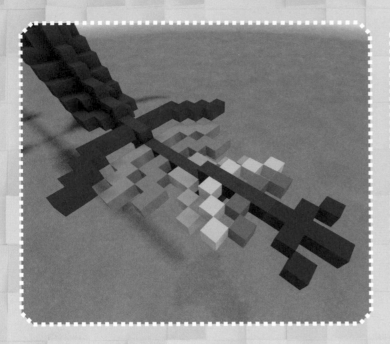

STEP 20

Get creative and decorate the dragon with rainbow colours. We decorated the tip of the tail and the dragon's snout! Then add white teeth inside the mouth.

STEP 21

Use some more white blocks to create spines running all the way along your dragon's back.

STEP 22

Start building a pair of strong back legs coming down from the dragon's body. Use the images above and to the right as a guide.

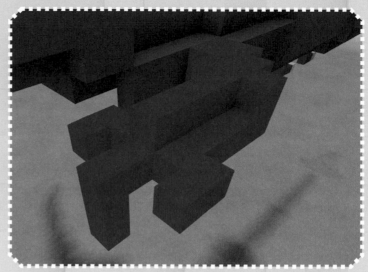

STEP 23

Now build the front legs – they are much shorter than the back ones. Give all the legs clawed feet by copying the shapes shown here.

STEP 24

When you're happy with your dragon's feet, add blocks in a contrasting colour to the tips of the claws. Yellow looks great with purple!

STEP 25

For the finishing touch, let's go truly technicolour with a rainbow underbelly! Make sure you do the same colour order as you've done elsewhere.

STEP 26

Keep your rainbow stripes going all the way along the bottom of dragon, right to the tip of its tail. You've created a multicoloured monster!

MULTI-HEADED

《 MONSTERS 》

There's only one thing scarier than a monster – and that's a monster with more than one head! Get to know a bit about these fearsome foes before embarking on your toughest challenge yet!

 ## THE HYDRA

According to Greek mythology, the Hydra is a nine-headed water monster that lives in the swamps. Immortal and super-ferocious, it's a creature best kept at a serious distance. But the most awesome thing about this beast is that when one of its heads is cut off, TWO more grow in its place!

⟪ ZMEY GORYNYCH ⟫

The famous dragon Zmey Gorynych appears in Russian fairy tales. Its name means 'Snake of the Mountains', and it's just as terrifying as you'd imagine. Zmey Gorynych is fierce, flying and fire-breathing. Depending on which story you read, this fearsome beast has three or more heads. In some tales, it can have as many as 12 heads!

⟪ YAMATA NO OROCHI ⟫

Here's a monster from Japanese mythology that has eight heads AND eight tails. This hulking creature is called Yamata no Orochi, which means 'eight-branched giant snake'. The legendary serpent-dragon is covered in moss and has glowing red eyes. It is SO enormous that trees grow on its back!

⟪ LADON ⟫

Meet Ladon, the serpent-like dragon from the Garden of the Hesperides. It was said to have up to 100 heads! According to Greek myth, Ladon was the guardian of the garden's golden apples and would twist its many hissing heads around a tree to protect them. This dragon was eventually defeated by the Greek hero Heracles during his quest to steal the golden apples.

YAMATA NO OROCHI

TEN THOUSAND WONDERS LEAP TO LIFE IN A FABULOUS, FUN-FILLED ADVENTURE!

COLUMBIA PICTURES presents

THE LITTLE PRINCE AND THE EIGHT-HEADED DRAGON

A TOEI PRODUCTION · A FULL LENGTH CARTOON FEATURE IN MAGICOLOR AND WONDERSCOPE

The Little Prince and the Eight Headed Dragon is a Japanese animated movie from 1963. In the film, a young prince called Susano-o battles **Yamata no Orochi** to save a princess.

ZMEY GORYNYCH

All of your dragon creations have been leading up to this supreme master build: the mighty multi-headed monster Zmey Gorynych! What could be more terrifying, or more challenging, than this?

MATERIALS

STEP 1

Begin by creating a grey toe shape, using the image on the left as a guide. Then start building the dragon's toe upwards, graduating the layers.

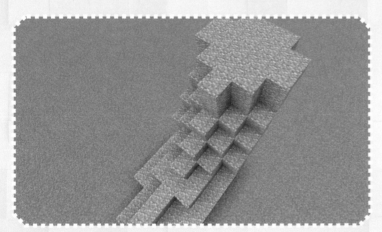

STEP 2

Now build two more toes in the same way, but make the middle toe the largest. Join them together as you build upwards to create a foot shape.

STEP 3

Now for the dragon's
leg. Start by forming the
ankle shape. Build
upwards and slightly
forwards. To create
a bend in the knee,
stack up a few blocks
vertically before
building up and back.

STEP 4

Keep building up
the leg, making sure
that it gets wider
the higher up the
thigh you go. Once
you have made the
leg the right length,
you can add more
grey blocks to play
around with the
shape and texture
of it.

STEP 5

Repeat steps 1 to 4 to
make a second leg for
your dragon. Be sure
that you have a large
enough gap between
the two feet so that
the legs won't touch.

Mark out a space before
building the second foot.

STEP 6

Join up the two legs by building the dragon's bottom, as shown above. As you can see from the picture in step 7 below, the legs need to look as though they're stuck onto the outside of the dragon's body.

STEP 7

Keep adding more grey blocks to form the dragon's rounded tummy.

Add layers of blocks, getting gradually smaller, to each side of the tummy. This will help you to achieve the round shape that you're aiming for!

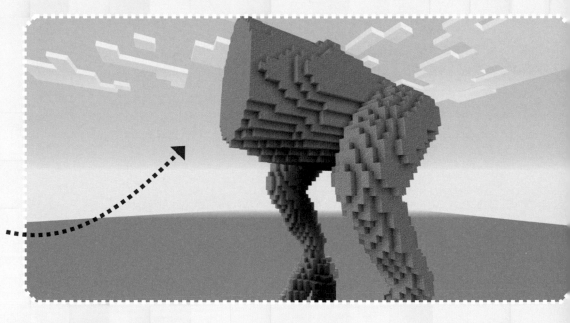

STEP 8

Continue to build up the dragon's body shape. This is what your dragon should look like from the front.

+

STEP 9

Turn your dragon round – it's time to create the tail. Build out from the back end to form the base of the tail. Make each new row a bit narrower.

+

STEP 10

Check out the pictures on the left and below for how to create the perfect pointed tail.

Make the tail curve around, like this.

Now Zmey Gorynych needs some front legs to go with its powerful back ones! Start by adding blocks to each side of the body for its shoulders. The front legs will be like a T-rex's arms – much smaller than the back legs.

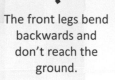

The front legs bend backwards and don't reach the ground.

STEP 12

Map out a rough shape for the front legs before filling them in with more blocks. Make sure they are bent backwards, as shown above. Finally, add three large claws to the end of each leg to create its fierce front feet.

Let's create the wings! First, build frames to help plan the size and shape. Make sure the wings match! If you get them right now, before you add the detail, it'll save you time later on. Check out the image on the right for inspiration!

STEP 14

Once you're happy with the shape of its wings, pick a second contrasting colour. We chose a reddish brown. Use this new colour to fill in the frame that you built in step 13. Keep layering so that it looks something like the image below.

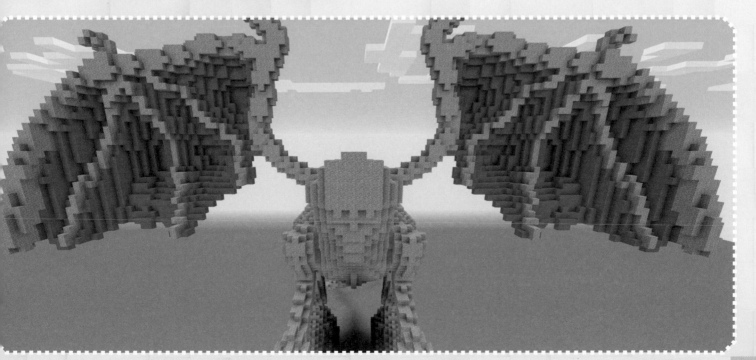

STEP 15

Create the dragon's first neck by laying more grey blocks out in a long straight line, as shown above. Keep adding rows of blocks to build up the shape.

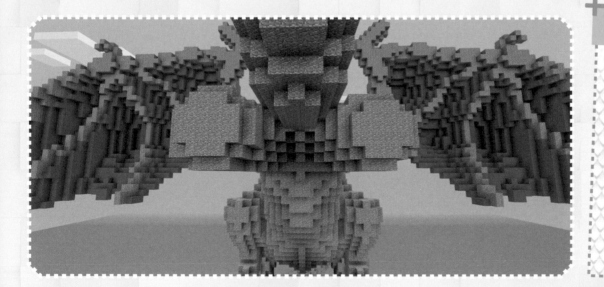

STEP 16

Nope, you can't move onto the head yet – you've got two more necks to build first! These necks should curve out from either side of the long middle neck you've just created.

STEP 17

Keep adding more grey blocks until your three necks look similar to the ones pictured on the right.

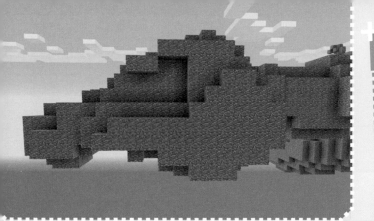

STEP 18

Now you can start on the heads! Give the dragon a long snout, leaving spaces for its eyes. You need to make three matching heads, so remember how you built the first one!

STEP 19

Now create an open mouth by adding a stepped lower jaw underneath the head. Leave enough room to add some big sharp teeth!

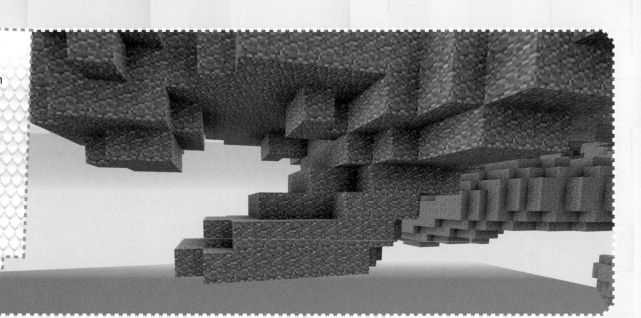

STEP 20

Use some white blocks for the teeth, then pop in some evil-looking eyes.

STEP 21

Choose a contrasting colour for your dragon's mane. We reckon this green colour works really well! Add as little, or as much, as you fancy.

When you're happy with the first head, repeat the process to create two more. Your mythical creature is really starting to take shape!

STEP 23

To make your dragon look extra awesome, why not add some colour to its belly? It looks best if you pick a colour that matches with the one you chose for the wings in step 14.

STEP 24

Now let's finish off those claws! Add white blocks to the tips of each claw on the front and back feet, as shown in the image above. This helps make the claws stand out and look super-sharp.

STEP 25

Congratulations, your Zmey Gorynych is done! Now you can have fun experimenting with different surroundings. This beast looks extra-terrifying in the dark. Check out those glowing eyes!

GLOSSARY

BLOCKS
Minecraft blocks are the main unit for building with and can be used in many ways. Some blocks are mined, while others spawn naturally.

ELEMENTAL
The dragon species that represent the powers of nature. These elements include water, fire, earth, and ice.

FOLKLORE
Old stories and beliefs of a culture or community that are passed down through generations, usually through word of mouth.

HABITAT
Natural home and territory of an animal or plant.

HERACLES
The Greek god best known for his strength and masculinity. Heracles' father was Zeus and his mother a mortal called Alcmene.

IMMORTAL
Everlasting creatures that don't die but live forever.

LEGEND
A very old and famous story that is retold from one generation to the next.

MYTHOLOGY
A collection of tales that a group of people tell to understand the world around them.

PRISMARINE
A decorative, stone-like block found underwater.

SCREEN SHARE
The way that computers allow you to share access to the same screen from two different locations.

SERPENT
Serpents or snakes are a symbol of mythology and represent both good and evil.

SKELETAL
The system of bones (skeleton) or framework that support a creature's body.

SUBHAVATSU
The old name for the river Swat in Pakistan, where a river dragon was said to live.

UNDERBELLY
The underside, or tummy, of an animal.

VENOMOUS
An animal that injects poisonous or toxic substances into its victims through biting or stinging.